SPORTS GREAT SHAQUILLE O'NEAL

Revised Edition

—Sports Great Books—

BASEBALL

Sports Great Jim Abbott
0-89490-395-0/ Savage

Sports Great Bobby Bonilla
0-89490-417-5/ Knapp

Sports Great Orel Hershiser
0-89490-389-6/ Knapp

Sports Great Bo Jackson
0-89490-281-4/ Knapp

Sports Great Greg Maddux
0-89490-873-1/ Thornley

Sports Great Kirby Puckett
0-89490-392-6/ Aaseng

Sports Great Cal Ripken, Jr.
0-89490-387-X/ Macnow

Sports Great Nolan Ryan
0-89490-394-2/ Lace

Sports Great Darryl Strawberry
0-89490-291-1/ Torres & Sullivan

BASKETBALL

**Sports Great Charles Barkley
(Revised)**
0-7660-1004-X/ Macnow

Sports Great Larry Bird
0-89490-368-3/ Kavanagh

Sports Great Muggsy Bogues
0-89490-876-6/ Rekela

Sports Great Patrick Ewing
0-89490-369-1/ Kavanagh

Sports Great Anfernee Hardaway
0-89490-758-1/ Rekela

Sports Great Juwan Howard
0-7660-1065-1/ Savage

**Sports Great Magic Johnson
(Revised and Expanded)**
0-89490-348-9/ Haskins

**Sports Great Michael Jordan
(Revised)**
0-89490-978-9/ Aaseng

Sports Great Jason Kidd
0-7660-1001-5/ Torres

Sports Great Karl Malone
0-89490-599-6/ Savage

Sports Great Reggie Miller
0-89490-874-X/ Thornley

Sports Great Alonzo Mourning
0-89490-875-8/ Fortunato

Sports Great Hakeem Olajuwon
0-89490-372-1/ Knapp

**Sports Great Shaquille O'Neal
(Revised)**
0-7660-1003-1/ Sullivan

Sports Great Scottie Pippen
0-89490-755-7/ Bjarkman

Sports Great Mitch Richmond
0-7660-1070-8/ Grody

**Sports Great David Robinson
(Revised)**
0-7660-1077-5/ Aaseng

Sports Great Dennis Rodman
0-89490-759-X/ Thornley

Sports Great John Stockton
0-89490-598-8/ Aaseng

Sports Great Isiah Thomas
0-89490-374-8/ Knapp

Sports Great Chris Webber
0-7660-1069-4/ Macnow

Sports Great Dominique Wilkins
0-89490-754-9/ Bjarkman

FOOTBALL

Sports Great Troy Aikman
0-89490-593-7/ Macnow

Sports Great Jerome Bettis
0-89490-872-3/ Majewski

Sports Great John Elway
0-89490-282-2/ Fox

Sports Great Brett Favre
0-7660-1000-7/ Savage

Sports Great Jim Kelly
0-89490-670-4/ Harrington

Sports Great Joe Montana
0-89490-371-3/ Kavanagh

Sports Great Jerry Rice
0-89490-419-1/ Dickey

**Sports Great Barry Sanders
(Revised)**
0-7660-1067-8/ Knapp

Sports Great Deion Sanders
0-7660-1068-6/ Macnow

Sports Great Emmitt Smith
0-7660-1002-3/ Grabowski

Sports Great Herschel Walker
0-89490-207-5/ Benagh

OTHER

Sports Great Michael Chang
0-7660-1223-9/ Ditchfield

Sports Great Oscar De La Hoya
0-7660-1066-X/ Torres

Sports Great Wayne Gretzky
0-89490-757-3/ Rappoport

Sports Great Mario Lemieux
0-89490-596-1/ Knapp

Sports Great Eric Lindros
0-89490-871-5/ Rappoport

Sports Great Steffi Graf
0-89490-597-X/ Knapp

Sports Great Pete Sampras
0-89490-756-5/ Sherrow

SPORTS GREAT SHAQUILLE O'NEAL

Revised Edition

Michael J. Sullivan

 Enslow Publishers, Inc.

40 Industrial Road   PO Box 38
Box 398   Aldershot
Berkeley Heights, NJ 07922   Hants GU12 6BP
USA   UK

http://www.enslow.com

Library of Congress Cataloging-in-Publication Data

Sullivan, Michael John, 1960–
    Sports Great Shaquille O'Neal / Michael J. Sullivan. — Rev. ed.
        p. cm. — (Sports Great Books)
    Includes index.
    Summary: Traces the personal life and basketball career of the center who began his
NBA career with the Orlando Magic in 1992.
    ISBN 0-7660-1003-1
    1. O'Neal, Shaquille—Juvenile literature. 2. Basketball players—United States—
Biography—Juvenile literature. [1. O'Neal, Shaquille. 2. Basketball players.
3. Afro-Americans—Biography.] I. Title. II. Series.
GV884.O54S94 1998
796.323'092—dc21
    [B]   98-18479
                                                                         CIP
                                                                         AC

Printed in the United States of America

10 9 8 7 6 5 4 3

To Our Readers:
We have done our best to make sure all Internet addresses in this book were active and
appropriate when we went to press. However, the author and the publisher have no control
over and assume no liability for the material available on those Internet sites or on other
Web sites they may link to. Any comments or suggestions can be sent by e-mail to
comments@enslow.com or to the address on the back cover.

Illustration Credits: AP/Wide World Photos, pp. 9, 10, 54, 57, 59; Barry Gossage,
pp. 27, 28, 30, 33, 36, 43, 47; Bob Greene/Paramount Pictures, p. 51; Brad
Messina/LSU, pp. 13, 15, 16, 17, 19, 21, 23, 49.

Cover Illustration: AP/Wide World Photos.

Contents

Chapter 1 . . . . *7*

Chapter 2 . . . . *11*

Chapter 3 . . . . *18*

Chapter 4 . . . . *26*

Chapter 5 . . . . *32*

Chapter 6 . . . . *48*

Chapter 7 . . . . *53*

Career Statistics *61*

Where to Write *62*

Index *63*

Chapter 1

A sellout crowd of over seventeen thousand filled the stands at the Los Angeles Forum on February 1, 1998. The game was going to be a big battle for Shaquille O'Neal and the Los Angeles Lakers. The opposition? The Michael Jordan-led Chicago Bulls! The Bulls had won the NBA championship the previous season, and O'Neal and the Lakers wanted to make a statement: They were going to challenge Chicago this year for the NBA title.

Several Hollywood celebrities were on hand to view this monster matchup between O'Neal and Michael Jordan. Among them were Jerry Seinfeld and Michael Richards of the television show *Seinfeld*. Actors Jack Nicholson and Dyan Cannon attended the event as well. Everyone could tell that this was a special game—one of eighty-two games, but a big one indeed. Even the normally late Los Angeles fans had already taken their seats before the opening tip.

The game was nationally televised by NBC-TV for the country to view. Broadcasters Bob Costas and Isiah Thomas were touting this game as a battle between the Lakers' newest sensation, Kobe Bryant, and Michael Jordan . . . but Bryant did not even start. You could not fool the Lakers' fans. They were eager to see Jordan try to score over O'Neal.

The Lakers' fans soon rose to their feet. After Scottie Pippen scored on a right baseline jumper to give Chicago the first basket, the Lakers worked the ball down low to O'Neal. O'Neal immediately faked to his left, causing his defender, Luc Longley, to also move left. O'Neal then quickly spun right and jumped up. Too late for Longley! O'Neal's shot was up in the air . . . swish! The game was now tied.

Jordan then took over for the next couple of minutes. His two jump shots and two dunks propelled the Bulls into a 14–7 lead. The Bulls were doing the same thing most NBA teams try to do when playing the Lakers. Teams usually try to surround O'Neal with two to three players. However, O'Neal knows when he has to be a team player. Several Bulls swarmed around him when he had the basketball about ten feet from the basket. O'Neal saw his teammate Rick Fox cutting to the basket. O'Neal tossed the ball to Fox, who made an easy shot. The Lakers crowd roared, appreciating O'Neal's passing.

O'Neal then helped ignite the Lakers crowd again, the next time Los Angeles had the ball. O'Neal had the ball at the foul line. He faked a move driving to the basket and stopped. His shot swished through the basket. The Lakers were now down by only one point. Jordan was determined to stop the Lakers' attack. He took the basketball and drove past two Lakers. Only O'Neal was left by the basket. Jordan went up to shoot over O'Neal. The shot was blocked by O'Neal! The Lakers then moved the ball down the court. The ball went inside to O'Neal. He was again surrounded by three Bulls. O'Neal quickly passed the ball to the running Derek Fisher, who scored on a layup. Game tied! The crowd roared! Chicago called time-out.

Shaquille O'Neal is being guarded by Scottie Burrell (24) and Dennis Rodman of the Chicago Bulls. Even though O'Neal was constantly double-teamed, he still managed to make fine plays.

O'Neal jokes on the bench with teammate Kobe Bryant (left). O'Neal had 24 points and Bryant scored 20 to rout the Bulls, 112–87.

That series of plays was just a few minutes of O'Neal at his best . . . playing against the best. The Lakers continued to rely on O'Neal and were able to forge a 57–53 lead. O'Neal had 15 points and 7 rebounds, to lead the Lakers in scoring and rebounding. It was going to get better. O'Neal and the Lakers completely smashed the Bulls in the third quarter, lifting the Lakers fans out of their seats on several occasions. After three quarters, the score was a lopsided 91–64.

O'Neal finished out the game with 24 points and 9 rebounds. He had a nice rest during the fourth quarter as his teammates wrapped up this very important victory, 112–87.

Chapter 2

Shaquille O'Neal was born on March 6, 1972, in Newark, New Jersey. Despite his above-normal adult size and weight, the newborn Shaq weighed in at just 7 pounds 11 ounces.

"My mother wanted me to have a first name that was unique," O'Neal later said, "and one day when she was looking through a book of Islamic names, she came upon it. Shaquille Rashuan, which means 'Little Warrior.' I was never little, but I was always a warrior."

The warrior in Shaquille kept his mother, Lucille O'Neal, his grandmother, Odessa, and his stepfather, Philip Harrison, very busy. (Shaq's biological father had left him and his mother shortly after Shaq was born.) Shaquille was like many other children—he was curious and wanted to explore the world. Even as a baby, he had a wonderful appetite. "I was a sneaky kid," he said. "My mother and grandmother used to hide extra bottles in my room. I was the kind of kid that used to hunt them down and drink them all!"

Shaquille's stepfather, who always believed in discipline, wanted his family to have a better standard of living than he himself had when he was growing up. So he joined the U.S. Army when Shaquille was just two years old.

Having Philip Harrison in the army was not very easy for Shaquille and his family. It meant they had to move around quite a bit. When Shaquille was halfway through the first grade, Philip Harrison was transferred to Bayonne, New Jersey. Shaquille's family now lived on an army base. They would live on bases until Shaq entered Louisiana State University (LSU) some eleven years later.

Shaq did not have much time to make friends. When he was in the third grade, his stepfather was transferred again. This time the family was moved to Eatontown, New Jersey, about fifteen minutes from the Jersey shore. Before Shaquille had a chance to get to know his new friends, his father was told he would have to move again. Now Shaq's new residence was down south—at Fort Stewart, Georgia.

By the time Shaquille was ten, it was becoming very hard for him to make friends. Because he was bigger than most of the other kids in school, people thought that Shaq was mean. Kids also made fun of his unusual name. He often ended up in fights at school. Then, when he got home, his mother and stepfather would punish him for his misbehavior.

By the time Shaquille was a teenager, though, he stopped fighting and took up dancing. "I was really good at it," he said. "I was never clumsy. I was never handicapped by my size. I think my parents were secretly proud of me. I probably inherited the ability from my mother, who is a very graceful woman."

Shaq used to do many types of dancing, including break dancing. He was finally starting to make some friends when, yet again, he had to move. This time, his stepfather was transferred out of the United States. Shaq said good-bye to all his sixth-grade friends and went with his family to Germany.

At the playground, O'Neal relaxes with some of his young friends. When O'Neal was young, he sometimes had trouble making friends because his family moved often.

It was a rough situation for Shaquille, who didn't know anybody there. But he still made his parents proud of him.

"I will say with some pride that I never got into drugs and alcohol," O'Neal said. "There were kids doing drugs, even on the army base, but that wasn't for me. I was always scared of dying from some kind of overdose—same thing with booze. I took a sip of beer once and the only word I can find for it is 'nasty.' I don't like the taste of it and I don't like what it does to you."

His stepfather's guidance molded Shaq into the kind, hardworking person he is today. "His father did a terrific job in keeping him in line," said Herb More, who was one of Shaquille's high school coaches. "Not only did his father do a terrific job but his mother was also a major factor. I think Shaquille ended up with his mother's personality.

"Shaquille, when I first met him, was one of the most incredible kids. He had such a warm personality and a great smile. He would light a room with his smile. He also has a terrific sense of humor. He should be proud and his parents should be proud of him. He turned out to be one terrific person."

Shaq did have his difficulties in Germany, though. By the time he was fourteen years old, he was six-feet seven-inches tall. Shaq suffered from Osgood-Schlatter disease, a disease that affects the bones of young people, especially boys. Shaq had it in his knees, and it was very painful. He had to rest, and drink plenty of milk to provide the calcium his bones needed to combat the disease. Slowly, the pain began to go away.

Shaq's biggest break in Germany was meeting Louisiana State University's head basketball coach, Dale Brown. Coach Brown was teaching a clinic for youngsters and the two instantly hit it off. They kept in touch after the clinic ended. Shaquille asked Brown for some advice on how to increase the strength in his legs and upper body. Brown recommended a Nautilus program and gave Shaq some literature to help him overcome his leg and upper-body weakness. Because of Shaq's size, Brown thought he was talking to a soldier! "I'm not in the army," Shaq told him. "I'm only thirteen." But what amazed Brown even more was that Shaq was not on his high school's basketball team.

In Shaquille's second year of high school in Germany, his stepdad was transferred back to the United States. The family was now living on an army base in San Antonio, Texas. Shaq tried out for the Cole High School basketball team. "When he walked into our practice I thought, 'Wow, this is some opportunity,'" Herb More recalled. "He was just great from

Shaq takes a breather during a game at Louisiana State University. As a teenager, he had a bone disease in his knees that forced him to rest and take time away from basketball.

day one. He was respectful. He was hardworking. He always listened to you. And he gave us input, too. He picked up the game real fast."

Shaquille started to impress people with his basketball skills. He began to gain weight and to improve his physical strength in his legs and upper body. He was now able to dunk without much difficulty and was beginning to perfect his monster slams.

"I remember in one particular game we were playing a rival school down here," More said. "The coach came over and said his team was going to beat us. We kind of laughed by the bench. Shaq was taking his warm-ups. But the real competitiveness came through with Shaq at that point. After Shaq finished his warm-ups, I told him what the coach said.

15

He just looked at me. Never said a word. But I got the message."

The ball was thrown down low to Shaquille, who spun toward the right baseline and slammed the ball through the basket. The force of the slam shook the basket and bent the rim. Play continued. Again the ball went down low to Shaquille, who faked right and dribbled left, then slammed the ball through the basket. The rim was bent again. "The third time Shaquille did the same thing and the other coach was complaining," More said. "But Shaq wasn't hanging on the rim. He was so intense that the force of his dunks bent the rim. They had to play on that bent rim the second half."

At the start of his senior year at Cole High School, Shaquille was one of the biggest names being recruited. It seemed that every college and university wanted him. But Shaquille still remembered the help that LSU coach Dale

The monster slam that brought Shaq attention in college was first perfected in high school.

16

O'Neal discusses strategy with a Louisiana State coach. O'Neal was recruited by every major university, but Louisiana State was always his top choice.

Brown had given him, so he ended the recruiting speculation early in his senior year by choosing LSU over schools like Kentucky, UCLA, North Carolina, Duke, Indiana, Michigan, and Ohio State.

"We were quite fortunate to get a player and a person like Shaquille O'Neal to come to our school," said Brown. "He had a terrific attitude. He always listened to you. He wanted to become the best basketball player he could. He gave us so many great memories here at LSU. It was great to have him here."

At LSU, O'Neal piled up the points and rebounds. In 1989–90, his first year there, he averaged close to 14 points a game and 12 rebounds. He also blocked 115 shots and shot a sparkling 57 percent from the floor. O'Neal was just getting ready to explode onto the college basketball scene.

Chapter 3

Shaquille O'Neal was ready for his sophomore year. He had gained confidence after his freshman year and was in tremendous shape for the start of his second. "He was college basketball's best player when he was a sophomore," LSU coach Dale Brown said. "He did everything for us that year. If people didn't know how great he was after his freshman year, they certainly knew after his sophomore season."

O'Neal finished his sophomore year as college basketball's leading rebounder, with 14.7 per game. He also shot 63 percent from the floor and scored almost 28 points a game. O'Neal was chosen Player of the Year by United Press International, the Associated Press, *Sports Illustrated*, and L.A. Gear. He also won the prestigious Tanqueray World Amateur Athlete of the Year Award.

O'Neal set an LSU home record for single-game scoring, with 53 points against Arkansas State on December 20, 1990. He also had 25 double-point, double-rebound games—another LSU record. Shaquille had a triple-double against Florida in

Though he is triple-teamed by the defense, O'Neal finds the room to put up a jump shot.

1991. He scored 31 points, pulled down 21 rebounds, and blocked 10 shots!

Because of O'Neal's terrific sophomore season, many basketball onlookers thought that he should leave LSU early and play in the NBA. Many also thought he should not risk an injury in college. The wise move would be for O'Neal to apply for the NBA draft. He would certainly be among the top three picks.

"I think he wanted to stay in college because of the education he was receiving," O'Neal's high school coach, Herb More, said. "His mother and father stressed that education is very important. And they wanted to see him get that degree. But O'Neal, being so big, is an easy target for an opponent. He was finding out that they were pushing him more, shoving him more, and being more physical with him. I think now, looking back, he would probably have considered leaving after his sophomore year."

O'Neal stayed at LSU for his third year. Opponents were becoming rougher with him, though, and O'Neal was not happy about it. Neither was his stepdad. "When you are the star, that's what happens," More explained. "Shaq has been getting pushed and shoved all of his basketball career. It was just getting a little too much during his last year at LSU."

Despite the pushing and shoving, O'Neal had another great year at LSU. He scored 24 points a game and was second in the nation in rebounding, with 14 per game. He had his best season in blocks, with 157 in 30 games in 1991–92. But Shaq was tired of the dangerous physical play in college. There was no doubt that he was going to be a star in the NBA. So why wait? "He made the right move leaving LSU to go to the NBA at that point," More said. "When you have a tremendous career ahead of you, why risk it by playing one more year in college?"

Shaquille O'Neal was ready for the NBA. Orlando had won the right to pick first in the NBA draft, held in Portland, Oregon, on June 24, 1992. There would be no question whom Orlando would pick. Just two minutes after the start of the NBA draft, Commissioner David Stern said, "The Orlando Magic select Shaquille O'Neal of LSU."

There was joy and celebration in Orlando, where ten thousand people had gathered to hear the announcement at the Orlando Arena. The Magic were going to be a real threat in the NBA because of O'Neal's talent and physical presence. O'Neal had now grown to 7 feet 1 inch, and 295 pounds. He signed a seven-year contract worth $41 million. Despite the large sum of money, O'Neal was humble about his good fortune. "I'm not about money," he said. "I'm not about seeing how many cars I can buy, or how many closets I can

Gliding to his left, Shaquille O'Neal moves past his defender. Standing seven feet tall, O'Neal was an easy target for aggressive opponents.

fill up with clothes. I make more money in one year than my father made in his entire life. But that doesn't make me a better person than him."

In O'Neal's first NBA game, an exhibition contest against the Miami Heat, he showed the fans why he was the league's No. 1 pick. He finished with 25 points, 6 rebounds, and 3 blocked shots. He was in fine form to begin his NBA career.

O'Neal's first regular-season game was on November 6, 1992. It was also against the Miami Heat, but this time in Orlando. O'Neal's superstitions started to form then. He remembered that once, before a game in college, he had eaten a slice of pizza and some pasta. That night, he had played really well—so he decided to continue the tradition when he made his NBA debut. It worked wonders for both the Magic and O'Neal. He scored 12 points, pulled down 18 rebounds, and blocked 3 shots to help Orlando win, 110–100.

O'Neal's first goal was to help the Magic improve over the previous season. In 1991–92, Orlando had won only 21 games. O'Neal wanted to play for a winning team. He hoped his presence was going to add more wins for the Magic, and indeed it did. Orlando finished O'Neal's first month in the NBA with victories over Indiana and Charlotte. The Magic were 8–3 after only one month with Shaquille O'Neal!

The next month was a rough one for the Magic. The team lost six straight games before finally defeating Philadelphia at home. O'Neal had 20 points and 15 rebounds in the game. He continued to excite the fans around the NBA with his slams and jams. In O'Neal's next game, against the Sacramento Kings, he was at his finest. He scored 22 points, pulled down 20 rebounds, and blocked 7 shots. He continued his assault on the Magic's NBA opponents with 28 points, 19 rebounds, and 5 blocks, in a win against Utah on December 22, 1992.

O'Neal was getting better each month. He had to improve

because he was playing against some of the best players in the world. "I knew I was a better player in January than I had been in November," O'Neal said.

Knicks center Patrick Ewing, considered one of the NBA's best players, was in town on January 8, 1993, to face the Magic and O'Neal. The Knicks and Ewing looked sharp in the first three quarters and were leading, 79–67. Ewing had scored 17 points while holding O'Neal to just 11 points. However, Orlando was now a tough team to beat at home because of O'Neal. He scored 11 points in the fourth quarter and blocked three of Ewing's shots in the last twelve minutes to help the Magic win an exciting 95–94 contest. Ewing had a chance to win the game in the last second. But guess who blocked his shot? Shaquille O'Neal!

The Magic met the challenge of the NBA World Champion Chicago Bulls and Michael Jordan in Orlando on

After three seasons at Louisiana State, O'Neal made the decision to turn professional. He was the top choice of the 1992 NBA draft.

January 12, 1993. O'Neal was the big reason for Orlando's win over Chicago. He scored 29 points and pulled down 24 rebounds!

The Magic stayed around the .500 mark for most of January and finished the month at 18–19. The team's record was a remarkable improvement over the previous season, when Orlando had won only 21 games the entire season. But O'Neal still was not happy. He would not settle for an average record. In the next game he scored 46 points against the Detroit Pistons, but Orlando still lost. This was becoming a problem for the Magic in O'Neal's first season. He would score 25 to 35 points a game but would receive little offensive support. The Magic needed an outside scorer to complement O'Neal's inside firepower.

O'Neal's first-half performance in 1992–93 was noticed by the fans around the NBA. He received 826,767 votes in the All-Star Game balloting, and outpolled Patrick Ewing for the starting center slot. O'Neal did not let his supporters down. He tallied 13 points in fourteen minutes of the first two quarters. However, he only played eleven more minutes in that game. The Eastern Conference team was coached by New York coach Pat Riley, who played his center, Ewing, for most of the second half.

O'Neal did not complain. He wanted to be ready for the second half of the season. The Magic were still playing well, finishing the month of February with a 26–25 record. Orlando had visions of making the playoffs for the first time, and O'Neal was the force behind that dream. The Magic team was steady throughout March, hanging close to the Indiana Pacers for the eighth and final playoff spot in the Eastern Conference. April was going to be the key month for Orlando. The Magic had to win most of their games to qualify for the NBA playoffs. On April 13, the Magic bashed the Milwaukee

Bucks, 110–91, to keep their playoff hopes alive. But the Philadelphia 76ers defeated Orlando in the following game, 101–85. From there, it got worse. The Magic then lost to the Cleveland Cavaliers, 113–110.

Time was running out for the Magic. O'Neal and his teammates were desperate, and they played that way in their 88–79 victory over the Boston Celtics. But they were still two games out of playoff contention. O'Neal continued to provide Orlando with scoring and rebounding. He had 20 points and 26 rebounds against the Washington Bullets on April 20. The Magic moved to within one game of the Pacers. Then they had to play the Celtics again. This time the Celtics got their revenge on O'Neal and the Magic. Boston crushed Orlando, 126–98.

Orlando needed to win its last two games, while hoping that Indiana would lose twice. The Magic defeated the New Jersey Nets and the Atlanta Hawks to close out the year. O'Neal scored 31 points and 18 rebounds, to help provide the win over the Hawks. Orlando finished at 41–41, a twenty-game improvement over the last year. O'Neal was named NBA Rookie of the Year.

Unfortunately for the Magic, Indiana also finished at 41–41. It was the fourth tiebreaker—Indiana had scored five more points in head-to-head confrontations with the Magic— that allowed the Pacers, rather than Orlando, to go to the NBA playoffs.

O'Neal's first NBA season had ended. Now more than basketball was waiting for the man who had become the NBA's most recognized player and personality.

Chapter 4

Shaquille O'Neal stepped onto the floor of the America West Arena in Phoenix, Arizona. The sellout crowd was silent for a moment, as if someone had said "Shh!" to the seventeen thousand Suns fans. They had not forgotten that in last year's contest at Phoenix the "Shaq Attack" had collapsed a basket after dunking. The crowd booed O'Neal as he made his appearance.

O'Neal could not be concerned with the boos. This was an important game for the second-place Orlando Magic. They wanted to move closer to the first-place New York Knicks in the Atlantic Division of the NBA. The Magic needed O'Neal, and on this night of December 19, 1993, he did not disappoint his team.

Suns superstar Charles Barkley was just a little bit too confident playing before the home crowd. He drove past his man along the left baseline and went up toward the basket.

There Barkley was greeted by O'Neal, who swatted the ball away like a tennis player hitting a serve. But defense was only a small part of O'Neal's game. He drove past Phoenix

With rim-rattling authority, Shaquille O'Neal throws down another slam dunk. O'Neal goes to the basket with such force that it is often best to just get out of his way.

center Mark West and went up toward the basket. He missed his shot but picked up the rebound. Barkley stood right in front of O'Neal, ready to block it. O'Neal faked his shot and Barkley jumped. With his long, powerful arms O'Neal extended the ball toward the basket. Dunk! "Oooh!" the crowd roared.

O'Neal continued his dunking exhibition to the gathering excitement of the fans. Once again he dunked over West. Then he started picking on the Suns' backup center, Oliver Miller. O'Neal faked moving to his right, and then spun toward his left. In one swift motion, he stretched out his right arm, basketball in hand, and slammed the ball through the basket! The dunk enabled the Magic to tie the Suns, 46–46, with 3:41 left in the first half.

O'Neal continued his assault on the basket in the second half, with several rim-rocking slams. In the last twenty-four

O'Neal warms up before a game. His positive attitude has always inspired his teammates to play their best.

minutes, his 36 points and 15 rebounds helped the Magic to a win. This was impressive, because the Suns were tough to beat on their home ground. Until O'Neal and Orlando snapped that streak, Phoenix had won 9 games in a row at home.

It was a big win for the Magic. Orlando was in the middle of a tough five-game West Coast road trip. Magic coach Brian Hill saw the trip as a test to see whether O'Neal and his teammates were good enough to play for the NBA championship. "We need to continue to play well and play together and we'll become a playoff team," Hill said. "Of course, we are certainly going to need Shaq every game."

Next, the Magic went to Sacramento to play the Kings. The Sacramento team had some injuries to its players, including center Duane Causwell. O'Neal was ready to take advantage.

It was not until the third quarter that O'Neal started to play well. He scored 12 of his 27 points in that third quarter, including three thunderous dunks over Kings center Wayman Tisdale. O'Neal hit six of seven shots, which pushed the Orlando lead to 17 points. The Magic beat the Kings, 97–91, to finish their West Coast road trip with 3 wins in five games.

O'Neal and Hill were disappointed that the Magic had lost fourteen points from their seventeen-point lead during one stretch of the fourth quarter. "I just missed some shots," O'Neal said. "If I had made those shots it would have made a world of difference." Added Hill: "We told them at halftime, you cannot relax against this team. The Kings will make a run at you."

This was an important change of attitude for the Magic. The Orlando players were no longer happy with just staying close to an opponent. Shaquille O'Neal was never satisfied with scoring 30 points and pulling down 15 rebounds if his

Calling for the ball, O'Neal tries to post up Celtics center Robert Parish.

team lost. O'Neal wanted to play well—but he also wanted his Orlando team to win while he was playing well.

O'Neal proved he was more than a scorer. He also pulled down a game-high 17 rebounds against the Kings and had 5 assists. He also played forty-five minutes—more than any of his teammates.

"Shaq is so important to the Orlando Magic," said Peter Vecsey, NBC's expert on the NBA. "He creates a lot of problems for other teams defensively with his offense and he's a force on defense. You have to earn your points when you go against Shaq."

The Magic finished their road trip 3–2, which also included a win over Portland. "Any time you come out to the West Coast and return 3–2, you've done a pretty good job," Magic coach Brian Hill said. "We need to continue to play well and play together and we'll become a playoff team."

There were times when the Magic lost, even though O'Neal was a terror on the offensive end. For example, back on November 19, 1993, he brought his offensive firepower to the famed Boston Garden. O'Neal was tremendous. He scored 41 points and had 10 rebounds, but the Magic lost to the Celtics, 115–106. In that game, O'Neal received some support from Anfernee (Penny) Hardaway (20 points) and Dennis Scott (16 points), but it was not enough. "That's the one thing that the Magic have done to improve themselves over the past year," Vecsey said. "They have surrounded Shaq with better players. They still can improve themselves and as they do, they will be a little bit closer to playing for the NBA championship."

The Magic appeared to be on the right track. With O'Neal's inside offensive scoring and his excellent defensive skills, Orlando had the strength at the center position to compete for an NBA championship.

31

Chapter 5

Sometimes respect is shown in a cruel fashion. For the 1994 All-Star Game in Minneapolis, O'Neal had received 603,346 votes, to outdistance Patrick Ewing once again for the starting center position. During the game, O'Neal was surrounded by three or four players whenever he got the ball. He could barely get a shot off. It was the ultimate sign of respect for O'Neal, but it was disappointing for him and the fans who had come to see him perform his magic.

But O'Neal did not have too much time to be disappointed. The Magic had played well in the first half of the 1993–94 season. Making the playoffs was a great possibility for Orlando, and O'Neal did not want to let that opportunity slip away.

The Magic hung tough throughout the season, and finished in second place in the Eastern Division behind the New York Knicks. It was a dream come true for the fans in Orlando. Before Shaquille O'Neal came along, they did not expect much. Now, in O'Neal's second year, the Magic found themselves in the NBA playoffs.

Under pressure from Felton Spencer of the Utah Jazz, O'Neal slides to his right and makes a layup.

Orlando's opponent for the first round was the Indiana Pacers. Pacers coach, Larry Brown, was one of the best. Indiana's strategy was simple. The Pacers would surround O'Neal and let the other Magic players try to hit the shots. It did not work in the first half of Game 1. After one quarter the Magic led, 26–20.

O'Neal showed the same offensive skills in the second quarter, and Orlando led, 54–42, at halftime. Brown realized that one half of basketball did not mean that the game was over. He told his Indiana team to continue to triple-team O'Neal.

The Pacers, led by Reggie Miller and Rik Smits, cut the Orlando lead to 74–66, in the third quarter. The constant defensive pressure on O'Neal began to take its toll. Several times in the fourth quarter, two or three Indiana Pacers would surround O'Neal. It forced him to be patient and try to find an open teammate. When he *did* find a teammate, the results were not always good.

Indiana slowly climbed back into the game late in the fourth quarter. Exhausted and dripping sweat from the wear and tear of playing against two or three Pacers at a time, O'Neal walked onto the floor for the final ten seconds of Game 1.

O'Neal's 24-point effort and 19-rebound performance had helped Orlando hold its 88–86 lead. Indiana had the ball, and did something amazing. Instead of trying to tie the game with the easier two-point shot, the Pacers' Byron Scott surprised everybody. He shot a three-pointer, and it was good!

The Magic players were shocked. It was a short best-of-five series, and it was dangerous for the Magic to lose the first game at home.

Orlando never got back on track after losing Game 1. In Game 2, O'Neal was hounded, surrounded, and harassed every time he touched the ball. Still, he remained patient. He moved the ball outside in an effort to find open teammates. Few of them could connect on the jumpers, with the exception of Hardaway, whose scoring kept the Magic in the game until the final seconds. O'Neal, who was also in foul trouble, scored a season-low 15 points, having faced triple-teaming most of the time. Orlando lost the second game, 103–101, and was one game away from the end of the season.

The Magic would have to win the next three games to move on to the second round. The Pacers big men stuck to their strategy. They pushed and shoved O'Neal down underneath the basket to tire him out. Even so, O'Neal was able to score 14 points in the first half. Orlando scored the last 10 points of the second quarter and led, 52–46.

After three quarters, Indiana pulled to within 72–68. There were still twelve minutes to play. The pressure on the other Magic players started to show. Their shots were not going in when O'Neal got the ball to them.

The Magic were in deep trouble. O'Neal picked up his fifth foul, with 9:22 left. He had to sit on the bench. If he fouled once more, he would be out of the game. Orlando was still leading, 78–70. But Indiana scored the next 14 points as O'Neal watched helplessly from the bench.

It was too late when O'Neal reentered the game. O'Neal scored the Magic's last basket of the season, but that was with 4:18 left. He finished with a team-high 23 points. Orlando was eliminated, 99–86, in three straight games.

Later that summer O'Neal joined the United States national team, known as Dream Team II. The team's mission was to win the 1994 World Basketball Championships, held in Toronto, Canada. O'Neal was one of the most dominant players on the United States team, which beat their opponents by an average of 37.8 points. In the gold medal game, the

Driving hard to the basket, Shaquille O'Neal shoots over the outstretched arms of Cleveland's Brad Daugherty.

United States easily defeated Russia, 137–91. O'Neal was named the tournament's most valuable player.

Going into the 1994–95 NBA season no one doubted that the Orlando Magic was a young team that would improve as time went on. In the off-season, the team brought in Horace Grant to help add some veteran leadership. Grant had won three championships as a member of the Chicago Bulls. His job would be to help take some of the rebounding burden off O'Neal's shoulders.

The addition of Grant and the fine play of Penny Hardaway allowed O'Neal to have perhaps the best season of his young career. O'Neal led the league in scoring, averaging 29.3 points per game. More important, the Magic cruised through the regular season. The team finished the year with a record of 57–25, the best in the Eastern Conference.

Orlando's opponent in the first round of the playoffs was the Boston Celtics. Boston was fired up. This would be the last year that the Celtics would play in the fabled Boston Garden, and the team was hoping to close the arena's doors with an NBA title. The Celtics, however, were no match for O'Neal and the rest of the Magic. Orlando easily defeated the Celtics in four games. O'Neal led the Magic in scoring, averaging 22.5 per game for the series. Included in that total was a superb performance in Game 4, when O'Neal poured in 25 points and grabbed 13 rebounds.

Next up for the Magic was the mighty Chicago Bulls. Prior to the end of the season, Bulls superstar Michael Jordan came out of retirement to try to guide Chicago to its fourth NBA championship. Basketball fans all over the world were eager to see the battle that Jordan and O'Neal would wage on the court.

In Game 1 both teams came out ready to play. Jordan was frustrated all night long by the intense defense provided by Nick Anderson of the Magic. Anderson limited Jordan to 19 points and made the play of the game. With the Bulls leading by one point late in the game, Anderson poked the ball away from Jordan and into the hands of Penny Hardaway. Hardaway passed to Grant, who threw down a monstrous slam dunk, sealing the victory for the Magic against Grant's former team. The final score was 94–91. O'Neal led his team with 26 points and 12 rebounds. Surprisingly, O'Neal also hit on 12 of 16 free throw attempts. With the game on the line, O'Neal hit 2 free throws to keep the score close enough for Anderson to provide his heroics.

The Magic were riding high after the Game 1 victory, but the Bulls came back strong in Game 2. Prior to the game,

Michael Jordan changed his uniform number from forty-five back to his old twenty-three. It looked as if the switch helped, as Jordan burned the Magic for 38 points. O'Neal finished with 25 points and 12 rebounds but was in foul trouble throughout the game.

With the series knotted at one apiece, the teams went to Chicago for Game 3. Comfortable on its home court, Chicago came out smoking. Jordan scored 31 points in the first half. Then, the Orlando defense shut him down in the second, and he managed only 9 points the rest of the way. Of Orlando's defensive effort O'Neal said, "We knew if we shut everyone else down we had a chance. I don't think Michael ever gets tired. He is a real Superman and I am a real Superboy." A superboy he was. O'Neal had another great game, scoring 28 points and pulling down 10 boards. Once again, O'Neal was surprisingly good at the foul line at a time when the score was close. He hit two free throws with 46 seconds left, which brought the Magic lead to 106–101, and took the wind out of Chicago's sails. The Magic went on to win the game, 110–101.

Chicago came to play in Game 4. The Bulls opened up a 17-point lead in the second quarter. The Magic, however, stormed back behind the hot shooting of Dennis Scott. A Scott three-pointer tied the game at 67–67 late in the third quarter, and the Magic kept it close into the final minutes. With less than two minutes to play and Chicago leading by only four, the Bulls' Toni Kukoc nailed a three-point shot that put the game out of reach. The game had been a subpar performance for O'Neal, who finished with 17 points and 5 turnovers. Because of foul trouble, O'Neal was limited to just ten shots in the entire second half. Chicago emerged victorious, 106–95.

O'Neal came back strong in Game 5. Playing his best

defensive game of the playoffs, O'Neal shut down the Bulls' attack in the second half. When all was said and done, O'Neal had blocked 5 shots, ripped down 20 rebounds, and added 20 points of offense. The Orlando players showed that they were a bunch of guys with a lot of heart. After a dismal first half, the Magic proved they belonged by roaring back and winning, 103–95. Said O'Neal of his performance and his goal for the next game, "My moves started falling, free throws started falling. So we just have to go for the kill [in Game 6] on Thursday."

The task would not be an easy one. O'Neal and his Magic teammates knew that the Bulls would not go quietly. Game 6 was a struggle from start to finish. The Bulls were trying desperately to win on their home court and force a seventh game. The Magic had other ideas. Though the score was close, Chicago was in control for most of the contest. As time went on it looked more and more as if the Bulls would emerge the victor.

Chicago's B. J. Armstrong hit a three-pointer with 3:27 remaining, which put the Bulls ahead, 102–94. Against a team like Chicago, an eight-point lead is tough to overcome. But the Magic did not panic. Orlando clamped down on defense and forced Chicago to turn the ball over and take bad shots. With 42.8 seconds left, Nick Anderson hit an 18-foot shot from the right baseline that put the Magic up 103–102, and never looked back. The Magic scored the final fourteen points of the game, and won, 108–102. Hardaway scored 21 points, Scott had 21 points as well, and O'Neal led the team, with 27 points and 13 rebounds. O'Neal put the finishing touch on the Orlando win with a slam dunk for his team's final points.

O'Neal was overjoyed by his team's performance. His team had been the first since 1990 to eliminate a Michael

Jordan-led team from the playoffs. "We're defying all the odds, playing together, winning," he said.

Next up for the Orlando Magic would be a showdown with Reggie Miller and the Indiana Pacers. The Pacers and Magic were no strangers to each other, having met in the playoffs in 1994. This time, though, the stakes were higher. The winners would find themselves in the 1995 NBA Finals.

As the series opened, it looked as if the matchup was fairly even. The Magic took the first two games of the best-of-seven-game series on their home floor. Orlando won Game 1 by the score of 105–101, and Game 2, 119–114. Likewise, the Pacers took Games 3 and 4 in Indiana. The Pacers won Game 3, 105–100, and Game 4, 94–93. This worked slightly in Orlando's favor. They held the home-court advantage as a result of finishing first in the regular-season standings.

In Game 5 in Orlando, the Pacers came out of the gates quickly. After the first quarter, Indiana led 30–18, and had made 67 percent of its shots. Then, O'Neal took over the game. He dominated inside, causing his defenders to try to stop him by fouling him. Indiana's starting center, Rik Smits, was in foul trouble throughout the game. His backup, Greg Kite, was completely dominated by O'Neal. He fouled O'Neal four times in ten minutes. O'Neal, with help from reserve guard Brian Shaw and shooting guard Dennis Scott, led the Magic to a 15-point lead by the middle of the third quarter.

Indiana came back, and by the end of the game the Pacers had a chance to win it. Pacers guard Mark Jackson missed a twenty-five-footer with six seconds left. Anfernee Hardaway grabbed the rebound, and Orlando held on for a 108–106 victory. O'Neal had an incredible game, ending up with 35 points and 13 rebounds. Said O'Neal, "We just wanted to come out, win at home, play aggressive and just keep the intensity real high." A similar performance in Game 6 could take the Magic to the NBA Finals.

The Pacers came to play, as the team set out to win this game at home and force a Game 7. Future Hall of Famer Reggie Miller came out firing. He connected on 3 three-pointers in the first six minutes. Miller had 20 points in the first quarter alone, and Indiana opened up a 31–20 lead. The Pacers never looked back, opening up a thirty-five-point lead in the second half. When the final buzzer sounded, the Pacers were ahead, 123–96. Miller finished with 36 points and angered the Magic with his trash-talking. O'Neal finished with 26 points and 6 rebounds and was furious with the Pacers' actions toward the end of the game. "Were not going to forget this," O'Neal said. "They were pointing fingers, talking, . . . I'm going to remember that [in Game 7] Sunday."

In Game 7, O'Neal came out as if he were a man on a mission. He made seven of his first eight shots, powering his way to 17 first-half points. Miller, on the other hand, was constantly bothered by the Magic defense. The Magic hounded Miller, allowing him very few open looks at the basket.

O'Neal dominated the inside. Hardaway and Scott lit up the scoreboard from the outside. Once the second half began, the Magic never let the Pacers get close. O'Neal finished with 25 points and 11 rebounds, and the Magic won, 105–81. Now the Magic would face the Houston Rockets in the NBA Finals.

Houston was the 1994 NBA champion and was now looking for a second consecutive title. Houston's star player, Hakeem Olajuwon, was considered by some to be the best player in the league and had been playing some of the best ball of his career. Since coming into the league, O'Neal had sought the advice of the gifted Olajuwon. Even O'Neal's coach, Brian Hill, knew of the respect that O'Neal had for the Rockets' center. "He considers him [Olajuwon] probably the greatest player in the game. It's going to be a heck of a challenge."

Game 1 of the 1995 NBA Finals started well for the Magic. O'Neal and company executed a sound game plan and opened up a twenty-point lead in the second quarter. The Rockets bounced back and cut the Orlando lead to eleven points at halftime, 61–50. The Rockets' Kenny Smith hit 5 three-pointers in the third period, and the Rockets battled back to take an 87–80 lead after three quarters.

The lead changed hands again in the fourth. O'Neal and Olajuwon put on an awesome display, scoring back and forth. O'Neal's hook shot in the lane gave the Magic a 106–102 lead. Olajuwon responded by hitting a hook shot of his own, and converting the foul shot on the play. Orlando's lead was cut to 106–105.

After another O'Neal hook shot, the Magic soon led 110–107. The Rockets turned the ball over, but Orlando's Nick Anderson was unable to hit some crucial free throws in the closing minutes. With 5.6 seconds to play, the score remained 110–107. Rockets guard Kenny Smith dribbled into the Magic's offensive zone and launched a three-pointer with 1:06 left. The shot was good, and the game went into overtime.

Houston's momentum carried over into the overtime period. The Rockets were a little too much for the Magic, and eked out a 120–118 win. O'Neal and Hardaway each scored 26 points in the losing effort. Olajuwon was the star of the game, scoring 31 points.

Orlando was never able to recover from the opening game loss. The Rockets won the next three games, sweeping the Magic, 4–0. O'Neal played honorably, averaging 28 points

O'Neal looks for an open teammate. Some opponents triple-team O'Neal to stop him from making one of his famous slam dunks.

per game for the series, but Olajuwon was just too much. Olajuwon averaged 32.8 points and 11 rebounds per contest, leading the Rockets to their second straight championship.

O'Neal felt that reaching the Finals was something to build upon. "This is our first time," he said. "This is a learning experience. I'm going to get here again before I retire. I'm going to get here many times."

After the series, the Magic players vowed they would be back. A team full of bright young stars, the Magic were already looking forward to next year. Magic forward Dennis Scott said, "We should be able to get out of the East again . . . assuming none of our guys fall off a cliff, we can be back."

O'Neal and the rest of the Magic came back from the off-season looking to prove that the team could make it back to the Finals. The team had high hopes, but those hopes would soon come crashing down. In one of Orlando's preseason contests, Shaquille O'Neal broke his thumb. He missed the first twenty-two games of the season.

Surprisingly, the Magic held their own without their big star. Anfernee Hardaway played excellent ball, and the Magic's record without O'Neal was 17–5. That was good enough for second best in the league. With a healthy O'Neal, the Magic were sure to make another run at the Eastern Conference championship. In his first game back, O'Neal scored 26 points and grabbed 11 rebounds. It was as if he had never missed a game.

The Magic enjoyed the best season in the history of the young franchise. The team set a club record for wins, finishing 60–22. Only the NBA record-setting Chicago Bulls had a better record in the Eastern Conference. Despite missing twenty-eight games during the season, O'Neal finished third in the league in scoring, at 26.6 points a game.

Orlando's opponent in the first round of the playoffs would be the upstart Detroit Pistons. A good young team, the Pistons were led by Grant Hill, the 1995 Co-Rookie of the Year.

The Magic had little trouble disposing of the Pistons. Although each game of the series was close at the half, the Magic would blow the Pistons away in the third quarter. The Magic won the first three games of the best-of-five series— the first time in franchise history that Orlando had swept a series. O'Neal led the team in scoring for the series, averaging 21 points per contest.

Orlando's opponent in the second round was the Atlanta Hawks. The Hawks were led by one of O'Neal's Dream Team II teammates, guard Steve Smith. Atlanta's coach was the legendary Lenny Wilkens. Wilkens has won more games than any other coach in NBA history.

On May 8, 1996, the two teams met in Orlando for Game 1. Because the Magic had won their opening series so easily, the team had not played since April 30. Some worried that the Magic would be rusty and would not come out ready to play. Instead the Magic dominated. O'Neal finished with a career-playoff-high 41 points. Hardaway added 32, and the Magic won 117–105. Game 2 was more of the same. Though O'Neal was aggressively double-teamed by the Hawks, he still scored 28 points. Nick Anderson chipped in 22, and the Magic cruised to a 120–94 victory.

For Game 3, the series moved to Atlanta. With time winding down in the game, the Magic were clinging to a 100–96 lead. With 1:46 left, Penny Hardaway tipped in his own miss, and the Magic led, 102–96. Atlanta inbounded, and Steve Smith tried to take the ball to the basket. O'Neal moved to challenge Smith and stuffed the shot, sealing the win for the Magic. The final score was 104–99, with O'Neal scoring

24 points. After the game, reporters asked O'Neal about a possible Magic sweep in Game 4. O'Neal said, "I'd like to get this over with, rest up, and watch the Bulls get tired playing the Knicks."

It was not to be. In Game 4, O'Neal had his poorest game of the 1996 playoffs to that point. He scored 19 points, but only made 5 of his 17 foul shots. Steve Smith scored 35 points for Atlanta, and the Hawks defeated the Magic, 104–99. After the game, O'Neal took the blame for the loss. "Tonight was my fault. I don't make excuses for missing shots. I just missed them." Then, O'Neal guaranteed victory in Game 5, to be played in Atlanta. He said, "Winning at home makes it all sweeter. I'll be ready to send all of the crybabies home."

Game 5 was a struggle. The game remained close until midway through the fourth quarter. With 5:42 left in the game, Orlando broke through the Atlanta defense, going on an 11–1 run. O'Neal finished with 27 points and 15 rebounds, as Orlando went on to win, 93–81. The series was over, and now the Orlando Magic would have to face the Chicago Bulls for the Eastern Conference crown. Orlando had defeated the Bulls in last year's playoffs.

This, however, was not the same Bulls team. Playing a full season, Michael Jordan had reclaimed his status as the best player in the world. The Bulls still had All-Star Scottie Pippen, and had added the league's leading rebounder, Dennis Rodman. The Bulls had crushed all opposition during the regular season, finishing with an NBA-record 72 wins. Despite all the hype, the Magic were confident. Hardaway told reporters, "It's just another challenge, and it's going to be a great one."

The stage was set for Game 1. The Bulls came out firing, and Orlando was stunned. Jordan scored 21 for the Bulls, and

Flying through the air, Shaquille O'Neal dunks over Billy Owens.

Dennis Rodman grabbed 21 rebounds. Chicago blew Orlando out, 121–83. Making matters worse, Orlando's starting power forward, Horace Grant, was injured in the game. O'Neal, who finished with 27 points, had this to say: "Am I disappointed? Yes. Am I worried? No. It's only one game."

O'Neal should have been worried. The Magic failed to win a game in the series, getting swept 4 games to 0. O'Neal played well, averaging 27.0 points per game, but Jordan and the Bulls were just too much for the Magic. Jordan averaged 29.5 points a game for the series. O'Neal had nothing but praise for the Chicago great. "Jordan is Jordan. That's why he's the best player in the world."

Next for O'Neal would be the busiest off-season of his career.

Chapter 6

Off the court, Shaquille O'Neal continues to lend his time and name in helping out many charity organizations. When he was a member of the Magic, O'Neal was known for his charity work throughout the Orlando area. O'Neal spent many hours serving food to the needy on the Thanksgiving and Christmas holidays. He also buys toys for the kids who do not have any during the holidays.

Despite his tireless work in Orlando, he has not stopped helping people since he became a member of the Los Angeles Lakers. He continues to volunteer as the National Spokesperson for Reading Is Fundamental. O'Neal urged all children to read a book every week. The 7-foot, 300-pound center was an imposing figure when he sat down with the children to read to them. And they certainly paid attention!

O'Neal also became involved in a project called Read a Book For Mom. From the months of May through August, children ages seven through eighteen are urged to read a book and write a one-page description of it. The winning youngsters receive hotel accommodations and tickets to watch O'Neal

O'Neal poses with some of his fans. Every year he makes several trips to schools to urge kids to get an education.

play in an NBA game. The mother of the winning child receives free flowers for one year. This event has been a very successful event for O'Neal. He takes a lot of pride in his relationship with his own mother and in her positive influence on his life.

"I do all of this for my family, not for me," O'Neal said. "My mother has a real big smile on her face because none of her kids have gotten into trouble, gone to jail, or done drugs. She has beautiful successful kids. And she doesn't want anything else."

O'Neal's mom and stepdad also have become famous through television commercials. Philip Harrison was featured in an MCI commercial, Lucille O'Neal did a commercial for Robitussin's "Dr. Mom" campaign. O'Neal's family was becoming known and was expanding.

In August 1996, Shaquille O'Neal became the father of a baby girl named Taheara. O'Neal was with his wife, Arnetta, during the birth. "I didn't know if he was ready to be a father," said O'Neal's mom. "But since then, I've changed my mind because I've found out that he is very serious about taking on that role. So I have all the confidence in the world that he's going to be a good father. Besides, he had good teachers."

O'Neal did not forget his "good teachers." He bought a two-story, seventeen-room house for his parents. His mom is now a secretary in O'Neal's company, called One-Al, Inc. O'Neal's mom spends her thirty-five-hour workweek paying the bills and answering the hundreds of pieces of fan mail that come O'Neal's way. "Some of my happiest times," O'Neal said, "are when my mom calls me. She tells me 'You can be the best basketball player in the world or the worst. I'll still love you.'"

In 1996, O'Neal and the Cyrk printing company created

TWisM Inc. TWisM stands for The World is Mine. O'Neal started the clothing company and printing facility to help the disadvantaged youth in the city of Compton, California. By hiring inner-city youth, O'Neal hopes to give the people of Compton hope and keep the youth off the streets. "Compton reminds me a lot of the city where I grew up," O'Neal said. "The negative images of this city are nothing compared to the good things it has to offer."

Shaquille O'Neal has found success in the entertainment industry as well. He had a leading role in the movie *Blue Chips*, and continued to build upon that experience. He was cast as the lead in the action-comedy movie, *Kazaam*, and the movie *Steel*. In *Kazaam*, O'Neal plays a rapping genie. In

Shaquille O'Neal is shown here with his *Blue Chips* costars, from left to right: Nick Nolte, Matt Nover, and Anfernee Hardaway. In the movie, O'Neal plays college star Neon Bodeaux.

Steel, O'Neal is cast as a futuristic superhero. Acting has been just one of many new experiences for O'Neal.

O'Neal has his own record label and has recorded several rap albums. Some of them have made it onto the *Billboard* charts. O'Neal is also a spokesman for Reebok and Pepsi, as well as for a group of O'Neal-trademarked snacks and toys. O'Neal knows the importance of being a businessman; he knows he can't play basketball all his life. Shaquille O'Neal's name will be heard on television and in the movies many years after he decides he doesn't want to play basketball anymore.

Chapter 7

The 1996 Summer Olympics were to be held in Atlanta, Georgia. Shaquille O'Neal was selected to be a part of the United States Men's Olympic Basketball Team. The team was known as Dream Team III and was once again expected to easily win the gold medal. Led by O'Neal, Reggie Miller, Hakeem Olajuwon, Mitch Richmond, and others, the United States whipped through the competition. In the gold medal game, the United States defeated Yugoslavia, 96–69.

While training with the Olympic team, O'Neal made headlines. He had been declared a free agent after the 1995–96 season. Most people expected him to re-sign with the Magic. Instead, O'Neal took his game, and entertainment career, to Los Angeles. On July 18, 1996, O'Neal signed a contract with the Lakers that would pay him roughly $121 million over the next seven years.

O'Neal said later that the reason for his move was that as a young boy, he had always dreamed of playing for the Lakers. Now he would become part of the tradition of great Lakers centers. In the beginning there was George Mikan, the NBA's

Beating Australian Mark Bradtke to the basket, O'Neal slams for an easy two. O'Neal was a member of the 1996 United States Men's Basketball Team that won the gold medal in Atlanta, Georgia.

first great star, who led the Lakers to five NBA championships when the team played in Minneapolis. Next came Wilt Chamberlain—Wilt the Stilt, as he was known to fans—who led the Lakers to the 1972 NBA championship. Then Kareem Abdul-Jabbar came to L.A. to be part of the five Lakers championship teams of the 1980s. Now O'Neal would try to help the Lakers recapture their former glory.

Lakers vice-president—and Hall of Fame player—Jerry West felt that O'Neal was a great fit for Los Angeles. West said, "When you combine the size and strength he has, it makes him an almost unstoppable force."

At the time of the deal, some questioned O'Neal's desire to win. The critics thought that O'Neal was more interested in moving to Los Angeles to further his rapping and acting careers. O'Neal said that he wants nothing more than to win a championship and get his first ring. He once said, "I have ten fingers and no rings. And I love jewelry."

Everyone was eager to see O'Neal in a Lakers uniform. However, there was still more to come for O'Neal in the off-season. In October 1996, he was selected by the NBA as one of the "50 Greatest Players in NBA History." O'Neal was the youngest player to be selected.

Everyone expected the Lakers to be a strong team. In 1995–96, they had won 53 games without O'Neal, but they were eliminated in the first round of the playoffs. The Lakers had already boasted two outstanding young guards, Eddie Jones and Nick Van Exel. They had a good rebounder in forward Elden Campbell. On draft day, they traded for eighteen-year-old high school sensation Kobe Bryant. Now they had added O'Neal to their group of great young players.

O'Neal was solid at the start of the 1996–97 season. He played well in November and dominated in December. He was named NBA Player of the Month for December, averaging 27.6 points and 12.6 rebounds per game. In February, O'Neal was slowed by a knee injury that caused him to miss 28 games. He returned just in time for the playoffs. Although he had missed 31 games during the season, he still finished the year averaging 26.2 points and 12.5 rebounds. The Lakers finished second in the Pacific Division, with a record of 56–26.

The Lakers would have to face the Portland Trailblazers in the first round of the 1997 Western Conference playoffs. Though he had only been healthy for a couple of weeks, O'Neal was sharp. In Game 1, he manhandled Blazers center Arvydas Sabonis. O'Neal scored a new career-playoff-high 46 points, and the Lakers walloped Portland, 95–77.

The teams split the next two games, and the series was 2–1 in L.A.'s favor. In Game 4, O'Neal scored 27 points and was an impressive 9 of 11 from the foul line. The Lakers won, 95–91. Now they would face the Utah Jazz in the second round. The Jazz featured league MVP Karl Malone, as well as John Stockton, the NBA's all-time leader in assists.

Game 1 of the Western Conference Semifinals against Utah was a tough one for O'Neal. He was in foul trouble most of the night, and he shot poorly as well. The Jazz dominated the game, winning 93–77. O'Neal was double- and triple-teamed and shot only 6 of 16 from the floor, finishing with 17 points. After the game he made no excuses telling a reporter, "I just missed the shots bro." He did, however, vow to make a strong showing in the next game. He reminded his doubters, "I always come back. Always come back. Always come back."

In Game 2, the Lakers put forth a much better effort. O'Neal solved his problems with the Jazz defense. With 5:52 left in the game, he made a devastating power move on Utah center Greg Ostertag. That basket cut the Utah lead to 94–93. With 1:56 left in the game, Utah's Jeff Hornacek made a jump

O'Neal pulls a rebound away from Arvydas Sabonis of the Portland Trail Blazers. In Game 1 of the 1997 NBA playoffs, O'Neal lit up the Blazers for 46 points.

shot, to give the Jazz a 101–96 lead. The Lakers came back, trailing 103–101. With time running out, the Lakers' Nick Van Exel had the ball and was about to hoist up a three-pointer at the buzzer to try to win the game. Malone reached in to knock the ball away as the final whistle blew. O'Neal had pounded Utah's frontcourt players on his way to 25 points and 12 rebounds. It was not enough. Karl Malone finished with 31 points, to lead the Jazz.

Game 3 was a better game for the Lakers, but a bad one for

O'Neal. O'Neal was in foul trouble throughout the contest and was ejected from the game. He finished with only 11 points but still pulled down 10 rebounds. O'Neal's teammates stepped up their games. Reserve guard Kobe Bryant scored 19 points, and Van Exel added 17 as the Lakers won, 104–84. Now the series deficit was cut to a 2–1 Jazz lead.

Annoyed with their own poor play, the Lakers had a terrible Game 4. Guard Nick Van Exel argued with Coach Del Harris, and the Lakers never got on track. Karl Malone cut through the Lakers' defense, finishing with 42 points. Utah's Bryon Russell chipped in 29 as the Jazz won, 110–95. Despite being slowed by a sore hip, O'Neal finished with 34 points and 11 rebounds. The Lakers were now just one game away from elimination. After the game, O'Neal was clearly bothered by the way the year was turning out. "What a crud of a season. I want to win the whole thing. That's all I want. I don't want MVP or player of the year or whatever. I want the ring."

The ring would have to wait. In Game 5, O'Neal found himself in foul trouble once again. With the game tied, 87–87, and almost twelve minutes remaining, O'Neal was whistled for his sixth foul. Now he would have to watch the rest of the game from the bench. With O'Neal out of the game, the Jazz pulled away. Karl Malone dominated the low post, scoring 32 points and hauling in 20 rebounds. The Jazz won the game, 98–93, and took the series, 4–1. Despite fouling out, O'Neal finished with 23 points and 11 rebounds. For the 1997 playoffs O'Neal averaged a solid 26.9 points per game, and 10.6 rebounds per game. Despite the effort, he would go home empty-handed.

O'Neal started the 1997–98 season with a flurry. He was named NBA Player of the Week for the week ending November 16. The Lakers were rolling, and O'Neal was the player his teammates always looked for in the clutch. After

Shaquille O'Neal is one of the brightest stars in the NBA. The Lakers hope that O'Neal can lead the team back to the NBA championship.

all, before the season he was chosen by his teammates to be the team captain. Then, O'Neal was badly injured for the third season in a row. An abdominal strain kept him out for twenty games. He missed the last week of November and the whole month of December.

When O'Neal returned to the floor in January, he came back better than ever. He was named NBA Player of the Month for January. He averaged 29.0 points per game and 12.8 rebounds per game during that time—not bad for someone who had missed five weeks. He played so well that he was selected to play in the 1998 All-Star Game for the sixth time in his six seasons. In the All-Star Game, O'Neal scored 12 points to go with 8 rebounds. On February 10, 1998, he scored his ten thousandth career point.

The Lakers finished the year 61–21—the second best record in the Western Conference. In the playoffs, the Lakers lost to Utah in the Western Conference Finals. The following year, they were swept out of the playoffs yet again—this time by the San Antonio Spurs.

By the 1999–2000 season, O'Neal and his teammates were more determined than ever to win a championship. They went on to post an NBA-best 67 wins that year. In the playoffs, they eliminated Phoenix, Sacramento, and Portland on their way to the NBA Finals against the Indiana Pacers. There, the Lakers defeated the Pacers in six games to finally claim the championship that Shaq had been chasing for so long. O'Neal scored 41 points in the title-clinching game and averaged 38 points and 16.7 rebounds for the series overall. He was the unanimous selection for Finals MVP.

When it was all over, O'Neal broke down and cried. "I've held the emotion for about eleven years—three years in college and eight years in the league," he said. "It just came out."

O'Neal looks forward to collecting many more championships in the seasons ahead.

Career Statistics

College

YEAR	TEAM	GP	FG%	REB	PTS	AVG
1989–90	Louisiana State	32	.573	385	445	13.9
1990–91	Louisiana State	28	.628	411	774	27.6
1991–92	Louisiana State	30	.615	421	722	24.1
Totals		90	.610	1,217	1,941	21.6

NBA

YEAR	TEAM	GP	FG%	REB	AST	STL	BLK	PTS	AVG
1992–1993	Orlando	81	.562	1,122	152	60	286	1,893	23.4
1993–1994	Orlando	81	.599	1,072	195	76	231	2,377	29.3
1994–1995	Orlando	79	.583	901	214	73	192	2,315	29.3
1995–1996	Orlando	54	.573	596	155	34	115	1,434	26.6
1996–1997	L.A. Lakers	51	.557	640	159	46	147	1,336	26.2
1997–1998	L.A. Lakers	60	.584	681	142	39	144	1,699	28.3
1998–1999	L.A. Lakers	49	.576	525	114	36	82	1,289	26.3
1999–2000	L.A. Lakers	79	.574	1,078	299	36	239	2,344	29.7
Totals		534	.578	6,615	1,430	400	1,436	14,687	27.5

GP=Games Played   AST=Assists   PTS=Points
FG%=Field Goal Percentage   STL=Steals   AVG=Points Per Game
REB=Rebounds   BLK=Blocks

Where to Write Shaquille O'Neal

Mr. Shaquille O'Neal
c/o Los Angeles Lakers
Great Western Forum
3900 West Manchester Boulevard
Inglewood, CA 90306

On the Internet at:
http://www.nba.com/playerfile/shaquille_oneal.html
http://www.shaq.com

Index

A

Abdul-Jabbar, Kareem, 55
Anderson, Nick, 37, 39, 42
Arkansas State University, 18
Armstrong, B. J., 39
Associated Press, 18
Atlanta Hawks, 25, 45–46

B

Barkley, Charles, 26, 28
Bayonne, New Jersey, 12
Billboard charts, 52
Blue Chips, 51
Boston Celtics, 25, 37
Boston Garden, 31
Brown, Dale, 14, 16–17, 18
Brown, Larry, 34
Bryant, Kobe, 8, 55, 58

C

Campbell, Elden, 55
Cannon, Dyan, 7
Causwell, Duane, 29
Chamberlain, Wilt "The Stilt," 55
Charlotte Hornets, 22
Chicago Bulls, 7, 8, 10, 23–24, 36,
    37–39, 44, 46–47
Cleveland Cavaliers, 25
Cole High School (TX), 14, 16
Compton, California, 51
Costas, Bob, 7
Cyrk printing company, 50

D

Detroit Pistons, 24, 45
Dream Team II, 35, 45
Dream Team III, 53
Duke University, 17

E

Eatontown, New Jersey, 12
Ewing, Patrick, 23, 24

F

Fisher, Derek, 8
Florida, University of, 18–19
Fort Stewart, Georgia, 12
Fox, Rick, 8

G

Grant, Horace, 36, 37, 47

H

Hardaway, Anfernee (Penny), 31, 35,
    36, 37, 39, 40–42, 44–46
Harrison, Philip, 11, 12, 50
Hill, Brian, 29, 31, 42
Hill, Grant, 45
Hornacek, Jeff, 57
Houston Rockets, 41–44

I

Indiana, University of, 17
Indiana Pacers, 22, 24, 25, 34–35,
    40–41

J

Jones, Eddie, 55
Jordan, Michael, 7, 8, 37–40, 46–47

K

Kazaam, 51
Kentucky, University of, 17
Kite, Greg, 40
Kukoc, Toni, 38

L

L.A. Gear, 18
Longley, Luc, 8
Los Angeles Forum, 7
Los Angeles Lakers, 7, 8, 10, 48, 53–60
Louisiana State University (LSU), 12,
    14, 16–17, 18–25

M

Malone, Karl, 56–58
Miami Heat, 22
Michigan, University of, 17
Mikan, George, 53–55
Miller, Reggie, 34, 40, 41, 53
Milwaukee Bucks, 24–25
Minneapolis, Minnesota, 32, 55
More, Herb, 13–16, 19, 20

N

National Basketball Association
  (NBA), 8, 19–20, 22–23, 29, 31,
  32, 36, 37, 45, 46, 50, 53, 55,
  58–60
  All-Star Game
    1993, 24
    1994, 32
    1998, 60
  Championship
    1972, 55
    1992, 23
    1995, 40–44
    1997, 7
New Jersey Nets, 25
New York Knicks, 23, 26, 32, 46
Newark, New Jersey, 11
Nicholson, Jack, 7
North Carolina, University of, 17

O

Ohio State University, 17
Olajuwon, Hakeem, 41, 42, 53
One-Al, Inc., 50
O'Neal, Arnetta, 50
O'Neal, Lucille, 11, 50
O'Neal, Odessa, 11
O'Neal, Taheara, 50
Orlando Arena, 20
Orlando Magic, 20, 22–25, 26–31,
  32–35, 36–47, 48, 53
Osgood-Schlatter disease, 14
Ostertag, Greg, 56

P

Pepsi, 52
Philadelphia 76ers, 25
Phoenix, Arizona, 26
Phoenix Suns, 26–29
Pippen, Scottie, 8, 46
Portland, Oregon, 20
Portland Trailblazers, 31, 56

R

Read a Book for Mom, 48
Reading Is Fundamental, 48
Reebok, 52
Richards, Michael, 7
Richmond, Mitch, 53

Robitussin, 50
Rodman, Dennis, 46
Rookie of the Year, 25, 45
Russell, Bryon, 58
Russia, Men's Basketball Team, 36

S

Sabonis, Arvydas, 56
Sacramento Kings, 22, 29–31
San Antonio, Texas, 14
Scott, Byron, 34
Scott, Dennis, 31, 38, 40, 41, 44
Seinfeld, Jerry, 7
Shaw, Brian, 40
Smith, Kenny, 42
Smith, Steve, 45, 46
Smits, Rik, 34, 40
Sports Illustrated, 18
Steel, 51
Summer Olympic Games
  1996, 53

T

Tanqueray World Amateur Athlete of
  the Year Award, 18
The World is Mine (TWisM), 50–51
Thomas, Isiah, 7
Toronto, Ontario, Canada, 35

U

United Press International, 18
United States Men's Olympic
  Basketball Team, 53
Utah Jazz, 22, 56–58

V

Van Exel, Nick, 55, 57–58
Vecsey, Peter, 31

W

Washington Bullets, 25
West, Jerry, 55
West, Mark, 28
Wilkens, Lenny, 45
World Basketball Championships
  1994, 35

Y

Yugoslavia Men's Olympic Basketball
  Team, 53